Steinbrenner

Quotes, Hits, & Legacy

George Steinbrenner's Own Words,
The Words of Those Who Knew Him,
His Most Infamous Acts,
& His Most Famous Accomplishments

By

Dan Fathow

Megalodon Entertainment, LLC.

Published by Megalodon Entertainment, LLC. (Metairie, LA USA)
www.MegalodonEntertainment.com

First Printing: July 2010

Copyright © 2010 Megalodon Entertainment LLC. All rights reserved.

Visit **MEGALODON ENTERTAINMENT LLC.** on the web at:
www.MegalodonEntertainment.com

ISBN: 1-61589-023-8
ISBN-13: 978-1-61589-023-1

All team names are trademark of Major League Baseball.

BULK INQUERIES: Quantity discounts are available on bulk orders of this novel for educational, fund-raising, promotional, and special sales purposes. For details, please contact www.MegalodonEntertainment.com

CHECK OUT MORE GREAT RELEASES FROM
MEGALODON ENTERTAINMENT LLC

FROM LEWIS ALEMAN,
BESTSELLING AUTHOR OF COLD STREAK

A 20-YEAR RACE THROUGH TIME...

AN AMAZON BESTSELLER

IF YOU COULD GO BACK IN TIME, WHO WOULD YOU SAVE?

"There is craftsmanship in Aleman's details; elaborate use of adjectival simile and metaphor ... stimulates ... memorable ... space-time research well done"

Dionne Charlet
Where Y'At Magazine
Feb 2010

"*Faces in Time* was an adventurous, fast paced, time traveling novel...loved the twists and turns...Lewis writes beautifully, his work is filled with great detailed descriptions...a great adventure. I haven't seen anything out like it."

La Femme Readers
December 12, 2009

WWW.LEWISALEMAN.COM
FACEBOOK.COM/LEWISALEMAN

Table of Contents

FAMOUS STEINBRENNER QUOTES

FAMOUS STEINBRENNER QUOTES

What better way to learn about a man than through his own words? George Steinbrenner was never at a loss for comment, and here are some of his most memorable quotes over the course of his long career, covering topics as diverse as leadership, his lifetime ban from baseball, free agency, charity, gambling, his illegal contribution to Richard Nixon's campaign, and how he'd like to be remembered.

ON HIS ROLE AS AN OWNER UPON FIRST PURCHASING THE NEW YORK YANKEES

"We're not going to pretend we're something we aren't. I'll stick to building ships."

ON HIS PERFORMANCE AS AN OWNER:

"I haven't always done a good job, and I haven't always been successful. But, I know that I have tried."

"I was often misquoted. I was supportive of my managers, even though they all may not think so."

"The reason baseball has its problems is that owners weren't involved 20 years ago... I'm an involved owner. I'm like Archie Bunker. I get mad as hell when we blow one."

"I haven't always made the right decisions."

"I think about the next season right away."

"Owning the Yankees is like owning the Mona Lisa."

"We plan absentee ownership as far as running the Yankees is concerned."

"I won't interfere as much as I did last year."

"If I don't get involved, we're not going to get better."

"They may call me the Boss, but in the end, to succeed as owner of the Yankees, you have to be a servant — a servant to the history and legacy of the Yankees."

"Our team played hard, but we let our fans down. We will do better."

"Nobody has won as many games as we have in the past seventeen years."

"If we look this bad next week, the players and coaches will hear about it."

"The screws are coming down tomorrow." (After a poor loss to the Mets in 1981).

"When I was younger, I was a bit impatient and I made a few moves and decisions that in retrospect I shouldn't have made. But I have tried to go back and rectify those moves and mistakes."

"I'm not getting my money's worth. We'll practice and practice until we get it right."

"I'm not going to let this continue much longer. I can't afford to be patient. I'll get involved, and you know what happens when I get involved."

"That's what you're in business for. You try to make a success."

"I don't like to hurt people. Sometimes I just...well, I guess I can't help it."

"If my players don't start producing there'll be more fireworks around here by the Fourth of July than anyone can imagine."

"It's an incredible achievement, particularly when I remember that when I bought the Yankees, we had trouble drawing 1 million to the stadium. We have the greatest fans in the world."

"It's not the end of the world. I'm mellow. I'm getting back to where I was before. Mellow." (After a particularly harsh loss.)

"I'll be an S.O.B. if I'm going to sit here and sign these paychecks and watch us get our ass kicked by a bunch of rummies."

"We know how to win."

"I'm not worried, but if they lose, that will be another story."

"We won 103 games during the regular season, and even I know that you're just not going to win it all every year. But our fans should be confident that we are already at work on improving our team for 2003. Will there be changes? Of course. But will these changes be made arbitrarily or unilaterally by me? Absolutely not."

"I never called a manager in the dugout to dictate who should play or to say that he'd made a mistake."

"I would not have gone with a [Derek] Jeter in the past. I think I've changed. I was too demanding. Too hasty."

"Go back to Day One in history. Look at your great generals. The ones who really got the stuff done were the ones the troops bitched about. It's the same in sports."

"My employees know I'm tough on them, and I am. I demand more of them than they think they're capable of. I don't know of any other way to lead. I'm not here to run a country club."

"I went through some tough times. I got suspended twice."

"I won't be active in the day-to-day operations of the club at all. I can't spread myself so thin. I've got enough headaches with my shipping company."

"I guess I am an S.O.B. to work for. I don't know if I'd want to work for me."

ON HIMSELF:

"When you're a shipbuilder, nobody pays any attention to you. But when you own the New York Yankees, they do, and I love it."

"In the end, I'll put my good acts up against those of anybody in this country. Anybody."

"I am tough. Sometimes I'm unreasonable. I have to catch myself every once in a while."

"I'm very happy. Satisfied, let's say."

"I'm really 95 percent Mr. Rogers and only 5 percent Oscar the Grouch."

"But why shouldn't I speak out? Don't you speak out in this country?"

"I don't have heart attacks. I give them."

ON LOSING THE 2001 WORLD SERIES TO THE DIAMONDBACKS:

""It was a tough loss, one of the toughest," Steinbrenner said. "But we will be back. Mark that down. We will be back. Who says this thing is over?"

On Losing to the Angels in 2002:

"There is an old Scottish proverb that says, 'I am wounded, but I am not slain. I shall lay me down and bleed a while, then I shall rise and fight again.' That should be the feeling of all of the Yankees today. As for me, my chin is not on my chest. And I don't want anyone on my team to have his chin on his chest, either. Particularly since Sept. 11, the Yankees have come to symbolize the spirit, strength and resilience of New York, and I am very proud of all we accomplished this year. We won 103 games during the regular season, and even I know that you're just not going to win it all every year. But our fans should be confident that we are already at work on improving our team for 2003. Will there be changes? Of course. But will these changes be made arbitrarily or unilaterally by me? Absolutely not."

On Losing the 2003 World Series to the Florida Marlins:

"Of course, I was disappointed, but we will be meeting soon to make whatever changes are needed to bring back a stronger, better team for New York and our fans. You can count on it."

ON LOSING TO THE RED SOX IN THE 2004 ALCS:

"I congratulate the Boston Red Sox on their great victory," Steinbrenner said. "I want to thank our loyal fans for their enormous support. Of course, I am disappointed because I wanted a championship for them and for our city. You can be assured, we will get to work and produce a great team next year."

ON LOSING TO THE ANGELS IN THE PLAYOFFS IN 2005:

"I congratulate the Angels and their manager on the great job they've done. Our team played hard, but we let our fans down. Our fans are the greatest in the world and I want to thank them for their amazing support throughout the season. We will do better."

ON LOSING TO DETROIT IN 4 GAMES IN THE PLAYOFFS IN 2006:

"I am deeply disappointed at our being eliminated so early in the playoffs. This result is absolutely not acceptable to me nor to our great and loyal Yankee fans. I want to congratulate the Detroit

Tigers organization and wish them well. Rest assured, we will go back to work immediately and try to right this sad failure and provide a championship for the Yankees, as is our goal every year."

ON THE 2009 WORLD SERIES CHAMPIONSHIP:

"Every World Series victory is special, but this one is especially sweet coming in the first year in our new home. This group will become legendary similar to the 26 world championship teams that preceded them."

ON WINNING:

"Winning is the most important thing in my life, after breathing. Breathing first, winning next."

"Second place is really the first loser."

A SIGN ON HIS DESK:

"Lead, follow, or get the hell out of the way."

A SIGN HE HAD POSTED ON THE PLAYER'S TUNNEL:

"There is no substitute for victory."

– a quote from Gen. Douglas MacArthur

MOTIVATING THE TEAM:

"You guys don't want it bad enough. You're not giving 100 percent. You guys are Yankees and you have to play like Yankees."

ON THE PRESS PORTRAYAL OF HIMSELF:

"If I believed half the things said about me, I wouldn't go home with myself."

ON HIS FATHER:

"As I have said many times - my father was a great fan of Bill Dickey's and he certainly loved the Yankees. I hope that he would be pleased."

"My father wasn't a believer in 'monetary allowances' for my sisters and me, so he set us up raising chickens. We sold the eggs to our neighbors…If one of our neighbors wanted a fresh chicken, then we also had to kill and dress the chicken. That chicken would run around with no head. Suddenly he'd flop down and you had to pick up the feathers. Every night we had to update the books on everything we sold, and the earnings were equally split three ways." "My best and worst boss was the same man – my father. He never – and I mean never – took 'I can't' for an answer. He taught me the value system that, to this day, I have continued to practice."

"He was the type of man who never worked for you. He was your father. I never went in and said, 'Dad, do this' or 'Do that.' I'd go in and say, 'Dad, what do you think about this? What can we do?' I really needed him."

"I don't think I ever could exceed my father's successes. He was a completely satisfied man, he knew what he wanted to accomplish and he accomplished it. I did do a lot, though, to try to please him."

"I hope that my father would have been proud of me, but you never know. I don't look back and think about how he would judge me. He was very happy when I bought the Yankees, and he very much enjoyed being a part of it."

"He never took 'I can't' for an answer."

ON HIS ILLEGAL CONTRIBUTION TO THE RICHARD NIXON CAMPAIGN:

"You commit a crime when you make an illegal contribution. I was one of many. I won't even dwell on it. It was an old law, an antiquated law. I got some very poor advice. And that's all I'm going to say."

ON NEW YORK:

"As I've always said, the way New Yorkers back us we have to produce for them."

"The only thing I care about is the Yankees fans. I could care less what the other people or detractors say. It really doesn't bother me."

"New Yorkers are strong people. They've got to fight in the morning to get a cab. They go to a lunch place at noon, they gotta fight to get a table or a stool off the counter. You have to give the city a team that's filled with battlers."

"The day I don't want to win for New York, that's the day I better get the hell out of the business."

"I want to thank our loyal fans for their enormous support. Of course, I am disappointed because I wanted a championship for them and for our city. You can be assured, we will get to work and produce a great team next year."

"When you're entrusted with a tradition, you've got to protect it."

"Think of those 50,000 people in the stands and everybody watching on TV. They are the most loyal and dedicated fans in sports."

"This is the greatest city in the world, and its people are the greatest people in the world. And I just hope they like me."

"Maybe the silk stocking guys don't like the way I run this ball club, but the little guy—the bartender, the guy pushing a cart, the cab drivers—they're the ones who need the Yankees. My involvement is not sipping cocktails in all the fashionable places. My involvement is in the roots of the city."

HIS APOLOGY TO THE PEOPLE OF NEW YORK FOLLOWING THE DISMAL 1981 WORLD SERIES PERFORMANCE:

"I want to sincerely apologize to the people of New York and to the fans of the New York Yankees everywhere for the performance of the Yankee team in the World Series. I also want to assure you that we will be at work immediately to prepare for 1982."

ON FREE AGENCY:

"I am dead set against free agency. It can ruin baseball."

MISCELLANEOUS:

"Don't talk to me about aesthetics or tradition. Talk to me about what sells and what's good right now. And what the American people like is to think the underdog still has a chance."

"Every single day of my life I try to do two things that I don't like doing: [eating] broccoli is one of them."

"I like every cab driver, every guy that stops the car and honks, every truck driver. I feed on that. That keeps me working hard to be able to afford to do the things that we do."

ON HIS SUSPENSION:

"I don't think that anybody should be suspended for life for anything, other than murder. How is it helping someone to say, 'You're done forever, your life's over'?"

"People keep coming up to me and asking, 'How does it feel to be banned for life?' Banned for life. I wasn't banned for life. There was never a word of suspension, probation or ban in that agreement. It was never meant to be part of it."

ON MANAGERS IN THE HALL OF FAME:

"I don't want to be in the Hall of Fame. I don't think owners should be."

"If they have an owners Hall of Fame, I'll consider it, but believe me, I don't want to be in the Hall of Fame. I don't belong there."

ON BASEBALL:

"Is it in the best interest of baseball to sell beer in the ninth inning? Probably not. The rule has got to be more clearly defined. And then some process should be set up where the judge is not also the appeals judge."

"Having people scream nasty things at you is part of sports. I've had my share of it. They pay their money, they can say what they want."

"Baseball is not just a sport anymore; we are a business. We are show business. To compete for the entertainment dollar, particularly in New York, you have to have more than nine guys playing baseball; you have to have an attraction. And I have tried to do the best job I possibly can to give my fans an attraction."

ON BABE RUTH:

"Ruth was probably the greatest athlete to perform in any sport. Never has there been anybody like him."

ON GAMBLING:

"You shouldn't have any betting in the locker room at all, whether it's baseball or it's horses. You can't beat the horses. You can't beat any kind of gambling because they have the odds."

ON BUSINESS:

"My dad never let me have an allowance. He gave me chickens. I had to feed them, gather the eggs, and sell them. I kept ledgers. I had to run it like a business. When I went off to military school, I sold the business to my sisters for too much, and they haven't liked me since."

"I take my last phone call at home at about 11pm."

"There is not enough [time] to accomplish everything you'd like to get done."

"I sold my egg company to my sisters for three times what it was worth. They've never liked me since."

"I detest bankruptcy. To me, it signifies failure – personal failure, corporate failure."

"Winning was everything. I don't care what they tell you."

On Leadership:

"If you can't sit in the saddle, you can't lead the charge."

"The rate of the pack is determined by the speed of the leader."

On Hard Work:

"If you haven't got a hernia yet, you ain't pulling your share."

On Humor:

"Don't ever get so serious that you can't laugh at yourself."

ON YANKEE STADIUM:

"The original Yankee Stadium will always be a cathedral of baseball, but everything changes."

ON THE SEPT. 11TH ATTACKS:

"Particularly since Sept. 11, the Yankees have come to symbolize the spirit, strength and resilience of New York, and I am very proud of all we accomplished this year."

ON CHARITY:

"I believe the good you do for others comes back to you. But if you do something good for some person and more than two people know about it—you and the other person, then you didn't do it for the right reason."

ON HIS FATHER/WHY HE LEFT COLLEGIATE COACHING

"He told me to get home and get busy. I wish I could have stayed in coaching. My father never asked that much, but when he did it was an order."

ON JOSE CANSECO:

"I don't know much about Jose Canseco. I've heard the accusations that he used steroids, but I can't comment on that. He's awesome, though."

ON HIS SONS TAKING OVER/IF HE WAS IN PARADISE DURING THE REPEAT WORLD SERIES WINS:

"If I was in Utopia? I don't know. I might for a while, until one of my sons was ready. It's time, though, for the young man to come on. The old man's tired."

ON BUD SELIG:

"I don't agree with that, going halfway around the world at the beginning of the season. But it does a lot of good for baseball and for Bud Selig and that's OK with me."

On Lou Piniella:

"I don't believe I gave Lou enough of a chance, OK? He was going to be a good manager, he is a good manager with Cincinnati, and he's a great person. But I think he learned from his experience with me, too. And I think he would tell you that."

On Yogi Berra:

"I don't want to rehash that. I liked Yogi very much, always did like him, will always like him."

"It's too bad about Yogi. I like Yogi very much. Nice person. Fine person."

On Davey Johnson:

"I like Davey Johnson as a manager. He did great things for the Mets; he manages with his own style."

On Why He Didn't Hire Former Mets Manager Davey Johnson:

"We chose to go within our own organization, though I think Davey would certainly have to be high on anybody's candidate list."

ON PETE ROSE:

"I like Rose as a person. He played with great passion. I think he made a tragic mistake. We all make mistakes. You forgive and you move on."

ON MUSIC:

"I like Tchaikovsky as much as the next guy, but in this area I think people would rather hear pops concerts, and good ones."

ON BILLY MARTIN:

"I would say our relationship really, and this may sound crazy -- we're pals."

"I loved Billy Martin. I thought Billy Martin would be a great manager. The one thing that hurt Billy Martin was personal habits."

"The next time you drive me to the wall, I'll throw you over it."

"I can't criticize Billy's style and personality. In many ways, it's a lot like mine."

"It sells newspapers when Steinbrenner fires Billy but not when Steinbrenner keeps Billy on his payroll for life, brings him back each time, tries to help him get himself going. I know that sometimes I make mistakes; I'm dead wrong. But then I go back and try to make it right."

"What do you mean try? If I want to fire you, I'll fire you."

ON REGGIE JACKSON:

"I never should have let Reggie Jackson go; letting him get away was a bad deal. Someday, I'll speak about how that happened, but I don't want to right now. It was nothing between Reggie and me or Reggie and the ball club. It was an outside situation that occurred."

ON WORKING LATER IN LIFE:

"I still go to the office every day. I can't say that I have actually slowed down very much. I'm actually in the best shape that I have been in for a very long time."

ON OWNING A TV NETWORK:

"I was never one for owning a TV network, per se. I didn't understand how big that would be. I'm not sure too many people did."

ON MIT:

"I wasn't smart enough to get into MIT, but I was a contributor and served on several committees there. They named a track after my father there."

ON PRESIDENT REAGAN:

"I'm so respectful that President Reagan gave me a pardon. I had applied several times, and finally he did it. President Carter didn't see fit to, but President Reagan did."

ON "INFORMED SOURCES":

"I'm tired of 'informed sources'; I'm tired of 'sources close to the Yankees.'"

ON ALEX RODRIGUEZ:

"In acquiring Alex Rodriguez, we are bringing to New York one of the premier players in the history of the game."

ON REGGIE JACKSON AND DAVE WINFIELD:

"In sports, you've got to be truthful, you've got to face your performance. And the truth is, Reggie always delivered in the World Series. Mr. October. Dave didn't. That doesn't mean Dave is a bad guy. He just didn't deliver."

ON DAVE WINFIELD:

"Let me ask you something Do you think Dave Winfield was liked by his teammates? You're nuts, if that's what you think."

ON THE DAVE WINFIELD FOUNDATION:

"So this is the reason I don't care when people write that I was picking on Dave. I wasn't picking on Dave the ballplayer, I was picking on Dave and his agent and a foundation where funds were, in my opinion, totally, seriously misused."

"Well, things started to pop up that led me to believe that it wasn't being operated for the purpose that it was supposed to be to benefit kids in New York. We had reason to believe that the money was being spent in ways that were ludicrous by any standards of a charitable foundation."

ON "STEINBRENNER SUCKS"

"Let me tell you what they don't know I didn't even stay. When they started the 'Steinbrenner sucks,' I said, 'Come on, let's go, let's get out of here.' I got in the car, went back into town and went to dinner. See how wrong they are? I didn't convene the coaches that night."

ON HIS OWN BASEBALL PLAYING EXPERIENCE:

"Once in a while, I played second base; once in a while, outfield. But those were just pickup games and softball leagues. So when I bought the Yankees, I tried to stay one pace ahead of the players."

ON RETURNING FROM SUSPENSION:

"My goal is not to run the team again. All I want to do is see the truth come out."

ON UMPIRES:

"The man, in my opinion, has had it in for the Yankees ever since I labeled him and several of the umpires as scabs because they worked the American League Games in 1979 during the umpires strike." (talking about Dallas Parks)

"I think American League umpires are intimidated by the National League umpires. I've seen it time and time again in the World Series."

ON LOCKER-ROOM DOUBLE STANDARDS:

"Of course, another question is why women's tennis and golf don't allow men in the locker room. They don't allow anybody in the locker room, because they don't want to be faced with that problem. I'd like to be the first male reporter who tries to get into the women's-tennis locker room."

ON LEE MACPHAIL OVERTURNING ON THE PINE TAR INCIDENT WITH THE ROYALS:

"If the Yankees should lose the Eastern Division race on the ruling of Lee MacPhail, I would not want to be poor Lee living in New York City. He better start house-hunting in Missouri, close to Kansas City."

ON EXPANSION TEAMS:

"Of course, expansion does water down your talent a little bit."

ON HIS LIFETIME BAN:

"The spirit of the agreement was that it wasn't supposed to be a ban. But within ten minutes of the time we signed it, Fay Vincent said, 'It is a permanent suspension.' That's a lie! The man lied!"

ON WATERGATE:

"There are things that have never come out on Watergate that someday will come out."

ON MERCHANDISING:

"This is what has to be understood: a lot of Yankees fans have spent big money supporting the Yankees, buying Yankee goods, and we don't get all that money."

ON YANKEE TRADITION:

"I have nothing against long hair, but wearing a Yankee uniform represents tradition. I think a Yankee should look well-groomed. After all, I'm paying the bills and issuing the paychecks around here and I feel a certain way about the Yankee tradition."

"I wouldn't sell the Yankees for anything. Owning the Yankees is like owning the Mona Lisa. You don't sell it."

"What happened in Cleveland will eventually happen to Yankee Stadium. We grow. We can hold on to traditions in certain ways, but we can't hold on to all of it forever. Look at the restrooms at Yankee Stadium: They're not good enough anymore. I go to the World Series at Yankee Stadium and see a long line of guys waiting to get into the men's room. Waiting! All I can do is say, 'Hey, guys, hang tough!'"

"Don't just drink from the gymnasium fountain. Drink from every fountain on campus."

"I don't want to see Yankees with long hair. I don't go for that crap."

"I'm like a fan. I live with the Yankees and I die with the Yankees."

"Before every home World Series game, I walk the restrooms of Yankee Stadium to make sure they're clean."

ON BUYING CHAMPIONSHIPS:

"When you start talking about the best team money can buy, the Red Sox have as many free agents as we do. They just didn't pay as much."

ON HIS STORY OF PUNCHING 2 ROWDY DODGERS FANS IN AN ELEVATOR DURING THE 1981 WORLD SERIES:

"I clocked them. There are two guys in town looking for their teeth."

ON PLAYERS:

"I like my race horses better because they can't talk to sportswriters."

"I've tried to trade [Ken] Griffey [Sr.], and no one wants him. We'll see who wants Mr. Baylor."

"I wish sometimes you could let go of some of the players instead of the manager, but that's not how the game is structured. We have some players who are not as good as they think they are."

"I don't mean to hang it on [shortstop Roy] Smalley. He tries, but it's just not good enough."

"It's okay for me to criticize my players because I sign the paychecks."

"I'm fed up with his attitude. [Don Mattingly] ought to realize his lack of hitting lately has killed us." (Responding to Mattingly skipping an optional practice)

"Well, people have heard that Rickey [Henderson] didn't get back for the two games tonight because he didn't know the strike was over. Well, I tell ya gang, you know, they're not all mental giants."

ON GEORGE S. PATTON:

"He was a gruff son of a bitch and he led through fear. I hope I don't lead through fear, and I would hope it was more love and respect, but maybe it isn't."

ON YANKEE MANAGERS:

"Billy Martin will manage the entire season." (Fired by late July)

"Gene Michael will be here when they re-do Yankee Stadium." (fired 1 year later)

"If he thinks talking about it will help him, that's his problem. I feel like a father scorned. I feel like I have a son who has done something wrong and isn't mature enough to admit it." (talking about Gene Michael 1 month before firing him)

"Bob Lemon will manage the entire season, win or lose." (fired 14 games later)

"Yogi Berra will be the manager for the entire year, win or lose, bad start or no bad start, no matter what." (fired 16 games later)

"His [Joe Torre's] job is on the line. I think we're paying him a lot of money. He's the highest-paid manager in baseball, so I don't think we'd take him back if we don't win this series."

"Joe Torre is special to me. He was fired in three places before we hired him. The Mets had fired him. People said he didn't know what he was doing. There was a headline in *The Daily News*: CLUELESS JOE. I never let him forget that."

ON HOW MUCH THE YANKEES WERE WORTH:

"That only matters if you're selling.... And I'm not selling."

ON HOW HE'D LIKE FOR PEOPLE TO REMEMBER HIM:

"He never stopped trying. That would be good enough for me."

REFLECTIONS ON STEINBRENNER'S LIFE

REFLECTIONS ON STEINBRENNER'S LIFE

From celebrities to former players to ex-managers, the people who knew Steinbrenner chime in on what he was like.

"There is nothing quite so limited as being a limited partner of George Steinbrenner's."

–JOHN MCMULLEN, A BUSINESS ASSOCIATE.

"The two of them deserve each other — one's a born liar, the other's convicted."

–BILLY MARTIN, LEGENDARY YANKEES MANAGER COMMENTING ON STEINBRENNER AND REGGIE JACKSON

Back in 1982, Goose Gossage, a reliever for the Yanks, referred to Steinbrenner as "the fat man."

"You know George M. Steinbrenner III is the center of all evil in the universe."

—BEN AFFLECK, ACTOR

"I think of the New York City Ballet as the Yankees without George Steinbrenner." "

—JOHN GUARE

"The owner of the New York Yankees, Mr. George Steinbrenner who I had the greatest respect for, I want to thank him for giving me the opportunity to win that special ring in 1996."

—WADE BOGGS, HALL OF FAME 3RD BASEMAN

"I never minded George Steinbrenner spending obscene amounts of money to put the best product on the field."

—JAY MOHR, ACTOR

"If there is one thing Steinbrenner is famous for besides his ability to manage a great baseball team, it is his ability to get himself into trouble. From being banned from baseball for life to feuding with and changing managers 20 times, Steinbrenner is no stranger to controversy. But what is even more remarkable, is his ability to bounce back and reclaim the team he worked so hard to promote."

—EVAN CARMICHAEL, FAMOUS ENTREPRENEUR

"I think he [Steinbrenner] had an impact on all of us. I think, for me personally, he had a more personal impact on me because he gave me an opportunity when everybody else said I was done and wasn't gonna play baseball again. He was the one that stood up and said yes he will and he'll play in New York and he'll play for the Yankees. I'll always be grateful for him as a man. The belief that he had in me. Even through some hard times, he still stuck with me. He guided me, and he gave me a lot of wisdom of never giving up and never quitting. He just shared some good things with me as a person…He was a leader; he was never a follower."

—DARRYL STRAWBERRY, STAR OUTFIELDER FOR THE METS AND YANKEES

"A strong work ethic and accountability were the hallmarks of being a Yankees employee."

—JEFF IDELSON, FORMER YANKEE PUBLIC RELATIONS, PRESIDENT OF THE HALL OF FAME

"The things that he did in his life that we don't know about are greater than even the most successful things that we do know about."

–RICK CERRONE, FORMER YANKEE MEDIA RELATIONS

"He was tough. He was demanding. He wanted your best all the time. He wanted to win all the time."

–DON MATTINGLY ON PLAYING FOR STEINBRENNER

"There was a discipline there from the beginning," Mattingly said. "He wanted certain things and it was always that way. ... He felt like you needed to look neat and clean."

–DON MATTINGLY ON STEINBRENNER'S INFAMOUS GROOMING DEMANDS

"George had gotten after me after I had hit homers in eight straight games. He came out and said I was being selfish and things like that. That kind of rubbed me the wrong way and that festered over time."

&

"His vision, passion and commitment to winning recharged the Yankees and revolutionized the game."

—DON MATTINGLY, STAR OUTFIELDER

REFLECTIONS ON STEINBRENNER'S LEGACY

Reflections on Steinbrenner's Legacy

"I am deeply saddened to hear the news of George Steinbrenner's passing. His vision, passion and commitment to winning, recharged the New York Yankees and revolutionized the game.

I remember a man driven to succeed. He was the owner, 'The Boss' and number one fan of the Yankees. Our relationship was built on mutual respect. I will never forget and always be grateful for how he treated me and my family both during my playing days and after I retired.

I will miss him very much and extend my deepest condolences to his wife, Joan, and all the members of the Steinbrenner family."

—Don Mattingly, Star Outfielder and Hitting Coach

"George was like a father figure to me. He treated me well, he treated me fair and he gave me a wonderful opportunity to play and manage the game we all love. George will be remembered as one of the most influential and renowned owners of a franchise in sports history. He leaves a legacy of winning and an unwavering passion for success. My wife Anita and I send our heartfelt thoughts and prayers to the Steinbrenner family and the Yankees organization. George was very special to me and I loved him.

"I'm deeply saddened by this. George meant a lot to me. I loved the guy. I have a lot or great memories with him and I'll always be appreciative of all the things he did for me and my family. He was a great man who took a Yankee team that was struggling under CBS and turned it into another dynasty. George will go down as the most influential and successful owner not only in baseball history but in all of sports. His legacy is going to go on forever. My heartfelt condolences to his wife Joan and his family. I share their sadness today."

–LOU PINIELLA, FORMER MANAGER

"George was The Boss, make no mistake. He built the Yankees into champions and that's something nobody can ever deny. George and I had our differences, but who didn't? We became great friends over the last decade and I will miss him very much."

–YOGI BERRA, FORMER YANKEES MANAGER

"It's a very sad day for those of us over in New York City. We have lost a great person—a great owner—a great motivator—a great believer. That turned a franchise into what he's turned the franchise into. And just also a great person. Very sad day for all of us that love New York and understood him. And as a player, and playing for him, and winning three championships, and being a part of the Yankee organization. We know that that day has to come, but it's a sad day because of what he believed in and what he stood for."

—DARRYL STRAWBERRY, STAR OUTFIELDER FOR THE METS AND YANKEES

"He had a real loyalty to people, even those people that he fired. Bill Martin is the perfect example."

—RICK CERRONE, YANKEES EXECUTIVE

"It's a difficult time, on a great day for baseball, the All-Star Game, something everyone looks to; a great man in baseball passed. He's meant so much to not only this organization, but to the game of baseball, and to all of us personally."

—JOE GIRARDI, YANKEES MANAGER

"He's more than just an owner to me. He's a friend of mine. He will be deeply missed. I think he's a father figure to everyone that was in our organization in the past or present, because he really took care of his players."

&

"He expected perfection."

–DEREK JETER, NEW YORK YANKEES TEAM CAPTAIN

"He was and always will be as much of a New York Yankee as Babe Ruth, Lou Gehrig, Joe DiMaggio, Mickey Mantle, Yogi Berra, Whitey Ford and all of the other Yankee legends.

"I have known George ever since he entered the game in 1972. He was my dear friend for nearly four decades. Although we would have disagreements over the years, they never interfered with our friendship and commitment to each other. Our friendship was built on loyalty and trust and it never wavered. We were allies and friends in the truest sense of the words.

"My wife, Sue, and I pass on our deepest sympathies to the Steinbrenner family, to the New York Yankees and to all of his friends. We will miss him, especially tonight when the baseball family will be gathered at Angel Stadium for the All-Star Game."

–BUD SELIG, MAJOR LEAGUE BASEBALL COMMISSIONER

[Steinbrenner's legacy would be making the New York Yankees] "into an absolute gold mine and a monster of power and success in baseball. He was one of the few who realized this was an iconic franchise, and he could turn it into something really special, and he did."

–FAY VINCENT, FORMER MAJOR LEAGUE BASEBALL COMMISSIONER AND ONE WHO HAD MANY PUBLIC BATTLES WITH STEINBRENNER

"George was a fierce competitor who was the perfect fit for the city that never sleeps — colorful, dynamic and always reaching for the stars."

–BILL CLINTON, THE 42ND PRESIDENT OF THE UNITED STATES OF AMERICA

"Judith and I express our deepest condolences to the entire Steinbrenner family and of course to the much larger, New York Yankees family. George was a friend of mine for over 30 years. He was truly the most influential and innovative owner in all of sports.

He transformed baseball and sports broadcasting with the *YES Network* and brought New York seven World Series. Beyond that, he made the Yankees a source of great pride in being a New Yorker. George Steinbrenner's Yankees represent the will to overcome all odds which is precisely the will New Yorkers display when meeting every challenge they face. George will be greatly be missed but his legacy will carry on in the hearts and minds of all baseball fans."

–RUDY GIULIANI, FORMER NEW YORK CITY MAYOR

"Like New York and like the Yankees, George Steinbrenner was a champion. He was someone about whom you can truly say that there will never be another one like him. When he bought the Yankees in 1973 the franchise was moribund and he quickly restored them to greatness. I, along with millions of Yankees fans, am thankful for the countless hours of joy we have experienced watching his team at the Stadium or following them on television and radio. He was a true New York icon. My condolences and best wishes go out to the Steinbrenners and the entire Yankee family."

–CHARLES E. SCHUMER, NEW YORK SENATOR

"I will always remember George Steinbrenner as a passionate man, a tough boss, a true visionary, a great humanitarian, and a dear friend. It's only fitting that he went out as a world champ."

–JOE TORRE, FORMER NEW YORK YANKEE MANAGER FOR 12 YEARS

"Today I join 1.4 million Bronxites, and Yankee fans across the world, in mourning the passing of a great man, 'The Boss,' George Steinbrenner. During his tenure as owner of the New York Yankees, Mr. Steinbrenner did everything in his power to create his own winning tradition in the Bronx, an effort that resulted in seven World Series championships. While other baseball fans were jealous of his success, Yankee fans, like myself, loved him for it. Both the Bronx and New York City have lost a giant today-in baseball and in charity-and my deepest condolences go out to the Steinbrenners and the entire New York Yankees family."

–RUBEN DIAZ JR., PRESIDENT OF THE BRONX BOROUGH

"Few people have had a bigger impact on New York over the past four decades than George Steinbrenner. George had a deep love for New York, and his steely determination to succeed, combined with his deep respect and appreciation for talent and hard work made him a quintessential New Yorker."

–MICHAEL BLOOMBERG, NEW YORK CITY MAYOR

"George has been a very charismatic, controversial owner. But look, he did what he set out to do — he restored the New York Yankees franchise."

—BUD SELIG, MAJOR LEAGUE BASEBALL COMMISSIONER

"Florida joins the New York Yankees and Major League Baseball in mourning the loss of unparalleled baseball icon George Steinbrenner. As the principal owner of the New York Yankees, George redefined the description of a chief executive. During his tenure, the Yankees won 11 American League pennants and seven world championships. He loved his family, his team, New York City and his home in Tampa, where he brought the Yankees to train each spring and his family's shipbuilding business, providing employment to many families.

"While the public face of George Steinbrenner was a demanding owner, he was extremely generous to others. Many acts of kindness were bestowed to those in need, with most of those acts going unnoticed except by those who benefited.

"I join with fellow Floridians in offering condolences to George's wife, Joan, sons Hal and Hank, and daughters Jennifer and Jessica, all of whom reside in Tampa."

—CHARLIE CRIST, GOVERNOR OF FLORIDA

"Me as much anybody, I've seen all sides of him, and I've known him pretty well. I prefer at this time to just remember the positive things, the relationship that we re-established, his accomplishments with the Yankees. When all is said is done and they evaluate everything -- the revitalization of a storied franchise and all the championships he won—he deserves to be considered for the Hall of Fame."

&

"Everybody goes through many stages in life. I hope people remember the later stages of his career. No one is without flaws or without tragedy. He had his difficulties. But when his life is remembered, I think he'll get more praise than anything. He's due that."

–DAVE WINFIELD, HALL OF FAME OUTFIELDER

"The passing of George Steinbrenner marks the end of an era in New York City baseball history. George was a larger than life figure and a force in the industry. The rise and success of his teams on the field and in the business marketplace under his leadership are a testament to his skill, drive, and determination. All of us at the Mets send our deepest condolences to his wife Joan, his sons Hank and

Hal, daughters Jennifer and Jessica, his grandchildren, and everyone at the Yankees organization."

—FRED WILPON, SAUL KATZ AND JEFF WILPON, THE NEW YORK METS

"He had a profound impact on the game of baseball, like it or not. He raised the bar for winning to an all-new level. He took a wilting franchise in 1973 and rather rapidly turned it into a worldwide brand. When you look at the body of work that George had over his 37 years in the game, he's certainly worthy of consideration."

—JEFF IDELSON, FORMER YANKEE PUBLIC RELATIONS, PRESIDENT OF THE HALL OF FAME

"He believed in his players, loved his players... The thing people don't realize is that he cares about people. You don't get a better person than Mr. Steinbrenner... Anyone who ever put on a Yankee uniform will have respect for him...all you saw in his eyes when he came to the clubhouse was he believed in the Yankee pinstripes."

—DARRYL STRAWBERRY, STAR OUTFIELDER

"I was greatly saddened to learn today of the death of George Steinbrenner. Everyone involved in the game had great respect for what the Yankees accomplished during his tenure, both on and off the field. George Steinbrenner shared the players' competitive drive: his goal was for his team to win.

I also had the privilege to work with him on matters involving America's Olympic athletes. He was extremely well regarded for his efforts on their behalf over the years.

I am glad that I had a chance to be a part of Baseball while George Steinbrenner was on the scene."

–DON FEHR, FORMER BASEBALL UNION PRESIDENT

"No matter what people thought of 'The Boss', he was the best owner in sports.....PERIOD!"

–DAMIEN WOODY, JETS RIGHT TACKLE

"How can you describe working for one of the most powerful men in the world? You can't. Him saying, 'Hey pal' to me on a consistent basis, means the world to me. He was the Babe Ruth of owners. As a historian of the game, I can tell you that's how Babe Ruth greeted kids too.

"The pain is instantaneous, because you know one of your best friends in the world you're never going to see again.

"I felt pain for not only me, but people like me that he took care of for a long time.

"To a lot of us he represented a father, a brother, an uncle and a friend all wrapped into one.

"He gave me life. He gave me life. Seeing his compassion for the less privileged let me know that I had a shot as a minority."

–RAY NEGRON, STEINBRENNER'S ASSISTANT FOR 38 YEARS

"Baseball will miss him. He did a lot of great things - and some not so great - but it's a sad day for baseball, no doubt about it. He was a winner, and he made the Yankees a winner. Any Yankee fan had to love George Steinbrenner because he put the best team on the field."

–DON ZIMMER, FORMER YANKEES COACH

"George Steinbrenner was too complex a person to adequately describe in a short statement, but he was a great friend of mine and he will be missed. His impact on the game cannot be denied."

–JERRY REINSDORF, CHICAGO WHITE SOX CHAIRMAN

"Somewhere in heaven, Billy Martin just got fired. RIP George Steinbrenner."

–MICHAEL IAN BLACK, COMEDIAN

"Through 25 years of service to the U.S. Olympic Movement, Mr. Steinbrenner's contributions to athletes and Olympic fans are second to none. From his work on the Steinbrenner Report, and his volunteer service on the USOC Board, to his Chairmanship of the U.S. Olympic Foundation, George has left an everlasting impact on the USOC, the athletes and American public."

–HARVEY SCHILLER, FORMER EXECUTIVE DIRECTOR OF THE USOC

"We are saddened to learn of the passing of George Steinbrenner.

"George Steinbrenner's passion for the game of baseball helped revive one of the game's most storied franchises, and in the process ushered in the modern era of baseball business operations. Mr. Steinbrenner understood and embraced the power of the players, and he put this knowledge to good use in establishing the Yankees as one of the sports world's most iconic brands.

"Our thoughts and prayers go out to the Steinbrenner family, his friends and the entire Yankees baseball family."

DAN FATHOW

–MICHAEL WEINER, MAJOR LEAGUE BASEBALL PLAYERS ASSOCIATION EXECUTIVE DIRECTOR

"He was a buccaneer. He was a throwback to the entrepreneurs of the later 19th century. It wasn't always pretty what they did, but they helped build America."

–GEORGE F. WILL, *THE WASHINGTON POST*

"I am deeply saddened by the death of George Steinbrenner. Our community has lost a grand and generous person who made a difference in ways large and small. With a larger-than-life personality, he leaves a lasting legacy in sports, business, and philanthropy. Many times he worked behind the scenes to help individuals and institutions - all to make Tampa a better place to live. He was a true community leader. By making Tampa the home for his family and the spring training home for the New York Yankees, he forever changed our community for the better. He cared about law enforcement and their families and his establishment of the Gold Shield Foundation will continue to positively impact lives. His dedication to the betterment of the youth in our community was unmatched. Mr. Steinbrenner's passing is a great loss to our city and to his family and friends. On behalf of the city of Tampa, I offer condolences and I ask our community to keep them in your thoughts and prayers. He will forever be missed."

—PAM IORIO, TAMPA, FL MAYOR

"I was not particularly surprised. I knew he had been ill. He probably had more of an impact on a baseball team than any other owner that lived. He took a franchise that was hurting under CBS and now it's the no. 1 brand in all of sports. I think he was the greatest PR man that ever lived. I was always amazed by his ability to get the Yankees in the paper every day."

—BILL GILES, PHILADELPHIA PHILLIES OWNER

"I would like to express my deepest condolences to the Yankees organization and the Steinbrenner family on the passing of George Steinbrenner. He was more than a legend in the world of baseball, he was a man with true global impact. Mr. Steinbrenner was also a co-owner of the Nets during their most successful period in the *NBA*. For new franchise owners like myself, he was a model of how to build a dynasty team and what can be achieved if you have enough heart and vision. He was an absolute original."

—MIKHAIL PROKHOROV, OWNER NEW JERSEY NETS

"George Steinbrenner is an American icon and was one of the preeminent owners in all of sports. A true champion with his own unique style, he held his team to the highest standards and demanded a title for Yankees fans each and every season. I will remember him as a winner whose passion and enthusiasm became part of the fabric of New York City. He was an inspiration and represented the essence of leadership."

—WOODY JOHNSON, CHAIRMAN NEW YORK JETS

"It was the second of my two face-to-face interactions with Mr. Steinbrenner. The first time, I was with Reggie Jackson and we ran into him as we were getting into the elevator. He said, 'Welcome to the team, son, we're happy to have you aboard.' Just like [on] *Seinfeld.*

"One thing I found really interesting was that when he came to Yankee Stadium, the word would spread very quickly. You'd be on the field or in the locker room and people would start talking: 'The Boss is here, the Boss is here.' It added to the Yankee mystique."

—AARON BOONE, YANKEE 3RD BASEMAN

"Today we mourn the loss of one of this country's most iconic sports figures. His impact on sports supersedes baseball and the New

York Yankees. His work on behalf of the U.S. Olympic Committee and in particular U.S. Olympic athletes continues to affect the way the USOC conducts business today. The Steinbrenner report in 1989 revolutionized the USOC's sport performance philosophy, and a generation of Olympians have benefited as a result. His influence on the U.S. Olympic Movement, his devotion to sport and the pursuit of excellence will forever be remembered."

–LARRY PROBST AND BILL HYBL, U.S. OLYMPIC FOUNDATION CHAIR AND PRESIDENT

"I had the privilege of serving on the National Football Foundation board of directors with George Steinbrenner for many years, and his service and commitment to our organization played a significant role in our ability to touch the lives of countless young student-athletes. From his playing days at Williams College to his coaching days at Purdue and Northwestern, it was clear that George Steinbrenner was a product of the gridiron. We will miss his passion for giving back to our sport, and our thoughts and prayers are with his family and friends."

–ARCHIE MANNING, LEGENDARY QUARTERBACK AND NATIONAL FOOTBALL FOUNDATION CHAIRMAN

"The passing of George Steinbrenner leaves a significant void in the fabric of the sports world and New York City. The thoughts and prayers of our organization are with the Steinbrenner and Yankees families. George's energy and his commitment and devotion to the Yankees were unmatched, and he was as generous and charitable a person as has ever been in sports. His was a unique, special and unforgettable presence."

–JOHN MARA, NEW YORK GIANTS PRESIDENT

"George Steinbrenner was a dynamic personality in sports and in business. He was the ultimate competitor in both worlds. All of us in the business of sports want to win; that is the objective. George personified that ambition. He and his good works will be missed dearly. George and my father had a special relationship; they were both good businessmen, and George loved the Yankees and my father loved the Giants."

–STEVE TISCH, NEW YORK GIANTS CHAIRMAN

"Who else could be a memorable character on a television show without actually appearing on the show? You felt George even though he wasn't there. That's how huge a force of personality he was."

–JERRY SEINFELD

STEINBRENNER BY THE NUMBERS

Steinbrenner by the Numbers

One clichéd phrase that holds true for George Steinbrenner is that no one can say they don't know how they feel about him. His personality and business methods either induced strong feelings of admiration or harsh dislike. Either effect makes it somewhat difficult to discuss Steinbrenner without a bias. However, the numbers do tell a story that Steinbrenner was certainly effective.

Chief Accomplishments

-7 World Series Championships

-11 Pennants

-THE WINNINGEST YANKEE OWNER

-THE WINNINGEST MLB OWNER

3,364 WINS / 2,583 LOSSES / 3 TIES= .566 WIN/LOSS % OVER 38 YEARS.

STEINBRENNER BOUGHT THE YANKEES FOR $8.8 MILLION IN 1973 (AMOUNT AFTER $1.2 MILLION RESALE OF INCLUDED PARKING GARAGES – TOTAL PRICE PAID $10 MILLION)

VALUE AT THE TIME OF HIS DEATH = $1.6 BILLION

-Steinbrenner increased the value of The Yankees by 18,182%.

-Inflation from 1973 to 2010 only accounts for a 409% increase.

Sports Illustrated Cover Stories

06/18/90 *The Young, The Old, and The Restless*

03/01/93 *George II*

03/31/03 *You Can't Have too Much Pitching*

---

38 YEARS OF THE STEINBRENNER REIGN

STEIN Yrs	Year	G	W	L	TIEs	W-L%	PLACE	Managers	Play-offs
38	2010	88	56	32	0	0.636	1st of 5	Joe Girardi (56-32)	
37	2009	162	103	59	0	0.636	1st of 5	Joe Girardi (103-59)	Won WS (4-2)
36	2008	162	89	73	0	0.549	3rd of 5	Joe Girardi (89-73)	
35	2007	162	94	68	0	0.58	2nd of 5	Joe Torre (94-68)	Lost LDS (3-1)
34	2006	162	97	65	0	0.599	1st of 5	Joe Torre (97-65)	Lost LDS (3-1)

33	2005	16 2	95	67	0	0.586	1st of 5	Joe Torre (95-67)	Lost LDS (3-2)
32	2004	16 2	10 1	61	0	0.623	1st of 5	Joe Torre (101-61)	Lost ALCS (4-3)
31	2003	16 3	10 1	61	1	0.623	1st of 5	Joe Torre (101-61)	Lost WS (4-2)
30	2002	16 1	10 3	58	0	0.64	1st of 5	Joe Torre (103-58)	Lost LDS (3-1)
29	2001	16 1	95	65	1	0.594	1st of 5	Joe Torre (95-65)	Lost WS (4-3)
28	2000	16 1	87	74	0	0.54	1st of 5	Joe Torre (87-74)	Won WS (4-1)
27	1999	16 2	98	64	0	0.605	1st of 5	Joe Torre (98-64)	Won WS (4-0)
26	1998	16 2	11 4	48	0	0.704	1st of 5	Joe Torre (114-48)	Won WS (4-0)

25	1997	162	96	66	0	0.593	2nd of 5	Joe Torre (96-66)	Lost LDS (3-2)
24	1996	162	92	70	0	0.568	1st of 5	Joe Torre (92-70)	Won WS (4-2)
23	1995	145	79	65	1	0.549	2nd of 5	Buck Showalter (79-65)	Lost LDS (3-2)
22	1994	113	70	43	0	0.619	1st of 5	Buck Showalter (70-43)	
21	1993	162	88	74	0	0.543	2nd of 7	Buck Showalter (88-74)	
20	1992	162	76	86	0	0.469	4th of 7	Buck Showalter (76-86)	
19	1991	162	71	91	0	0.438	5th of 7	Stump Merrill (71-91)	
18	1990	162	67	95	0	0.414	7th of 7	Bucky Dent (18-31) and	

								Stump Merrill (49-64)	
17	1989	16 1	74	87	0	0.46	5th of 7	Dallas Green (56-65) and Bucky Dent (18-22)	
16	1988	16 1	85	76	0	0.528	5th of 7	Billy Martin (40-28) and Lou Piniella (45-48)	
15	1987	16 2	89	73	0	0.549	4th of 7	Lou Piniella (89-73)	
14	1986	16 2	90	72	0	0.556	2nd of 7	Lou Piniella (90-72)	
13	1985	16 1	97	64	0	0.602	2nd of 7	Yogi Berra (6-10) and Billy Martin	

								(91-54)	
12	1984	162	87	75	0	0.537	3rd of 7	Yogi Berra (87-75)	
11	1983	162	91	71	0	0.562	3rd of 7	Billy Martin (91-71)	
10	1982	162	79	83	0	0.488	5th of 7	Bob Lemon (6-8), Gene Michael (44-42) and Clyde King (29-33)	
9	1981	107	59	48	0	0.551	4th of 7	Gene Michael (48-34) and Bob Lemon (11-14)	Lost WS (4-2)
8	1980	162	103	59	0	0.636	1st of 7	Dick Howser (103-59)	Lost ALCS (3-0)
7	1979	16	89	71	0	0.556	4th	Bob	

		0					of 7	Lemon (34-31) and Billy Martin (55-40)	
6	1978	16 3	10 0	63	0	0.613	1st of 7	Billy Martin (52-42), Dick Howser (0-1) Bob Lemon (48-20)	Won WS (4-2)
5	1977	16 2	10 0	62	0	0.617	1st of 7	Billy Martin (100-62)	Won WS (4-2)
4	1976	15 9	97	62	0	0.61	1st of 6	Billy Martin (97-62)	Lost WS (4-0)
3	1975	16 0	83	77	0	0.519	3rd of 6	Bill Virdon (53-51) and Billy Martin (30-26)	

2	1974	162	89	73	0	0.549	2nd of 6	Bill Virdon (89-73)	
1	1973	162	80	82	0	0.494	4th of 6	Ralph Houk (80-82)	

THE DAVE
WINFLIED
SAGA

THE DAVE WINFIELD SAGA

Steinbrenner caused a stir in the sports world in 1981 when he signed outfielder Dave Winfield to a $23 million dollar, 10-year contract, which made Winfield the highest paid player in baseball at the time (It is an estimated equivalent of about $55 million in today's economy).

As for Winfield being worth the money he was paid, his Hall of Fame career stats speak for themselves. He is the 19th All-Time Career Hit Leader; he smashed 465 home runs to become 31st all-time (205 HRs in his 8 years with the Yankees, averaging 25.6 HRs per season with NY), and he drove in 1,833 RBIs (818 with the Yanks). Batting, Winfield is a career .283 hitter, and a .290 with the Yankees. Other honors included Winfield being selected for the All-Star Game during every year that he was in New York, and he was awarded 5 Gold Gloves for his play in the field (won 7 during his career). It is reported at baseball-reference.com that Winfield only received $14.29 million of his $23 million contract. While Steinbrenner made waves by signing the unprecedented high-salary contract, Winfield was a consistently solid player, eventually being named the 3rd Best All-Around Athlete of All-Time in Any Sport by ESPN. Steinbrenner's controversial deal was a smart decision. However, his treatment of Winfield was not.

Supposedly the rift between Steinbrenner and Dave Winfield stemmed from Steinbrenner mistakenly thinking he signed Winfield for $16 million instead of the $23 million. Whatever the impetus was, Steinbrenner was after Winfield during his entire play with the Yankees, eventually leading to catastrophe for the team owner.

One of the first public incidents involved Winfield's poor performance in the 1981 World Series versus the Los Angeles Dodgers, following his magnificent performance in the American League Division Series.

In 1981, Winfield only played in 105 games for his new team due to the strike, but he still put up a .294 batting average. However, Winfield batted an impressive .350 in the 1981 American League Division Series, including a triple and two doubles, helping put the Yanks past the Milwaukee Brewers. To put this performance into perspective, it was against a Brewers pitching staff lead by a 14-4 Pete Vuckovich with a .778 win percentage and the legendary closer Rollie Fingers with a 1.04 ERA and 28 saves on the year. The competition's batting was also strong with Cecil Cooper at .320 (4th in the AL), Robin Yount at .273, and Paul Molitor and Jim Gantner both at .267. Getting past the Brewers was certainly no easy task.

However, in the World Series, Winfield went 1 of 22 for a dismal .045 Batting Average. When Winfield finally got his only hit in the series, he asked if he could keep the ball, making a joke at his own expense. This gesture infuriated Steinbrenner, and resulted in public criticism from the owner.

In June 1984, Steinbrenner tried to trade Winfield to the Texas Rangers, but league rules prohibited trading a player who has

10-and-5, meaning a player who had been in the majors for at least 10 years and at least 5 with a single team. This would not be the last time Steinbrenner would try to find a way to trade Winfield.

Winfield's response to the attempted Rangers trade was, "The fact that he even thought of trading me shows the kind of mentality which is the reason we're in the position we're in now."

At the end of the 1984 season, Yankee teammates Don Mattingly and Dave Winfield were battling neck and neck for the batting title. The race was so close and so evenly matched that their performance in the last game of the season would decide the champion. Steinbrenner was quite vocal about who he wanted to win the race, Don Mattingly. Many of the fans seemed to favor Mattingly too, feeling that Winfield was not pulling his weight, being paid roughly 90 percent more than Mattingly. Mattingly was also a young rookie battling the star veteran, which made him a bit of an underdog.

Tensions began to rise, and Winfield refused to pose for a photo with Mattingly, explaining his stance with, "You want to know why I don't want any part of it? Because they are turning this thing into a racial thing, pitting teammate against teammate, black against white. It's gotten so they're even trying to split the clubhouse up on it."

In the final game of the season versus the Detroit Tigers at home in Yankee Stadium, Mattingly bested Winfield by going 4-for-5 earning a .343 average to the veteran's .340.

It would seem that having 2 players competing for the batting crown on the same team would be a publicity dream for the team's management. What could be better than promoting that they have the best 2 players in baseball fighting for the batting title up to the last game of the season in front of a home crowd at legendary Yankee Stadium? Somehow Steinbrenner thought it a better idea to try to slight Winfield than to take the above angle. Steinbrenner's willingness to pursue the vendetta at his own expense instead of promoting the talent on his own team is simply baffling.

Some people, including teammate Don Baylor, have tried to explain that the favoritism toward Mattingly as being based in racism. Traditionally, baseball fans of the 70s and 80s cared very little for race. Hank Aaron and Willie "The Say Hay Kid" Mays hold a special place in the heart of every baseball fan, and they played and were accepted decades before Winfield. And to further illustrate the point, just across town, two of the most popular and exciting players on the New York Mets and all of baseball were Darryl Strawberry and Dwight "Doc" Gooden. How could the same New Yorkers love Strawberry and Gooden, essentially blind to race, but suddenly and inconsistently be racist toward Winfield?

So, if the New York fans weren't likely to be racists conspiring against Winfield, could the racist have been Steinbrenner? If Steinbrenner's record illustrates one thing clearly, it's that he is an equal-opportunity grudge holder. He had no problem firing baseball legends Billy Martin and Yogi Bera, and he also had no qualms with feuding with Don Mattingly in the years to come.

In 1985 Steinbrenner uttered this widely publicized quote to Murray Chass of the *New York Times* about his highly-paid star outfielder, “Where is Reggie Jackson? We need a Mr. October or a Mr. September. Winfield is Mr. May.”

Teammate Don Mattingly defended Winfield by saying this about Steinbrenner making that comment, “To belittle players like he did, to me he’s out of control.”

Winfield’s response was, “You wonder why we’re tentative on the field. All I can tell you is that with what he said, with the way he is, that’s how the guys felt. Maybe some of the guys were too afraid to make a mistake.”

Fast forward a few years, and Winfield missed the entire 1989 season due to an injury.

On July 30, 1990, MLB Commissioner Fay Vincent banned George Steinbrenner from baseball for life. The charge was that Steinbrenner had hired Howie Spira for $40,000, a gambler with reported mafia connections, to dig up dirt on Dave Winfield. Winfield would be traded mid-season to the Angels, and Steinbrenner would be reinstated in 1993.

Steinbrenner and Winfield would not talk for over a decade after that.

The Reconciliation in the Words of Dave Winfield

"Ten years after I left, not a spoken word, not an olive branch, nothing. But in around 2000, 2001, I don't recall the circumstances that brought us together, but we got together in New York City and we talked and laid things out on the table that had never been said before. He apologized to me for the things that he did. It's almost like you see a curtain drawn back, a veil lifted, just a complete change. And our relationship changed from then on, and we got to know each other real well.

"I know that over the years, he admired me, he respected me and he liked me. And I did the same with him. It was very important. I poured out my life, my heart and soul to the ball club and to the city of New York, trying to accomplish the ultimate, to win a championship. But nevertheless, I know I gave everything I had every day I was there. And at the time, there wasn't a supportive environment. It was kind of negative. But I emerged from that a strong person and a better person.

"I've said many times, if a person wasn't focused, they might have crumbled under the circumstances. But I'm glad that I have a piece of calm that, as two men, we were able to come to terms and talk and respect one another. So I'm comforted with that respect."

"I don't want to have bad feelings about anybody in life, I really don't. He and I went from one extreme to the other, and we're just going to leave it on a good note with him today. He'll be missed as an icon in this sport, in this game. The history of the sport is gone. Let's just remember good things about him."

DAVE WINFIELD MLB CAREER STATS

YEAR	R	HITS	HR	RBI	B.A.	OBP	SLG
1973	9	39	3	12	0.277	0.331	0.383
1974	57	132	20	75	0.265	0.318	0.438
1975	74	136	15	76	0.267	0.354	0.403
1976	81	139	13	69	0.283	0.366	0.431
1977	104	169	25	92	0.275	0.335	0.467
1978	88	181	24	97	0.308	0.367	0.499
1979	97	184	34	118	0.308	0.395	0.558
1980	89	154	20	87	0.276	0.365	0.45
1981	52	114	13	68	0.294	0.36	0.464
1982	84	151	37	106	0.28	0.331	0.56
1983	99	169	32	116	0.283	0.345	0.513
1984	106	193	19	100	0.34	0.393	0.515
1985	105	174	26	114	0.275	0.328	0.471
1986	90	148	24	104	0.262	0.349	0.462
1987	83	158	27	97	0.275	0.358	0.457

1988	96	180	25	107	0.322	0.398	0.53
1990	70	127	21	78	0.267	0.338	0.453
1990	7	13	2	6	0.213	0.269	0.361
1990	63	114	19	72	0.275	0.348	0.466
1991	75	149	28	86	0.262	0.326	0.472
1992	92	169	26	108	0.29	0.377	0.491
1993	72	148	21	76	0.271	0.325	0.442
1994	35	74	10	43	0.252	0.321	0.425
1995	11	22	2	4	0.191	0.285	0.287
Career	1669	3110	465	1833	0.283	0.353	0.475

Stats with The New York Yankees

Years	R	Hits	HR	RBI	B.A.	OBP	SLG
1981-1988	722	1300	205	818	0.290	0.356	0.495

CUT THAT HAIR, YOU HIPPIE!

THE DON MATTINGLY AFFAIR

CUT THAT HAIR, YOU HIPPIE!:

THE DON MATTINGLY AFFAIR

This incident plays out in the real life-imitating-art category. It all begins with an all-star baseball guest cast episode of *The Simpsons*, entitled "Homer at the Bat," written by life-long baseball fan and long-time Simpsons scribe, John Swartzwelder. The original airdate of the episode was February 20, 1992. During the episode, Mr. Burns, Homer Simpson's boss and owner of the nuclear power plant, hired professional baseball ringers to win a softball game. Throughout the episode, Mr. Burns constantly told Don Mattingly, one of the hired softball ringers, to shave his sideburns. Part of the joke is Mattingly appeared with no sideburns at all, shaved all the way up to his hairline. The exchanges between Burns and Mattingly went like this:

Round 1

Mr. Burns : Mattingly, Get rid of those sideburns!

Mattingly : What sideburns?

Mr. Burns : You heard me, hippie!

Round 2

Mr. Burns : Mattingly, for the last time, get rid of those sideburns.

Mattingly : Look, Mr. Burns, I don't know what you think sideburns are, but...

Mr. Burns : Don't argue with me—just get rid of them!

Round 3

Mattingly arrives, his sideburns shaved up almost to the top of his head.

Mr. Burns : I thought I told you to trim those sideburns! Go home! You're off the team for good!

Mattingly : Fine…I still like him better than Steinbrenner.

The episode aired in Feb 1992, but it was written a year before. The real-life incident between Mattingly and Steinbrenner's grooming policy took place in 1991, after *The Simpsons* script had been written. So, this wasn't a case of *The Simpsons* directly lampooning Steinbrenner. It was a case of Steinbrenner's grooming policy imitating an already-written *Simpsons* script.

Another strange twist to it all is that this occurred during Steinbrenner's ban from baseball resulting from him paying Howie Spira $40,000 to dig up dirt on Dave Winfield. Most seemed to believe that Steinbrenner was still pulling the strings of the Yankees organization from behind the scenes, despite his ban, and had ordered that Mattingly get a haircut or sit the bench.

Mattingly refused to cut his hair. He was benched for a few games, and the media ran with the story, widely mocking the grooming policy of the Yankees. Mattingly soon returned to fulltime play, and the issue subsided.

The other MLB guest stars in "Homer at the Bat" were Wade Boggs (future Yankee), Ken Griffey, Jr., Steve Sax (Yankee), Roger Clemens (future Yankee), Ozzie Smith, Mike Scioscia, Jose Canseco, and Darryl Strawberry (future Yankee).

DON MATTINGLY CAREER STATS

YEAR	R	HITS	HR	RBI	B.A.	OBP	SLG
1982	0	2	0	1	0.167	0.154	0.167
1983	34	79	4	32	0.283	0.333	0.409
1984	91	207	23	110	0.343	0.381	0.537
1985	107	211	35	145	0.324	0.371	0.567
1986	117	238	31	113	0.352	0.394	0.573
1987	93	186	30	115	0.327	0.378	0.559
1988	94	186	18	88	0.311	0.353	0.462
1989	79	191	23	113	0.303	0.351	0.477
1990	40	101	5	42	0.256	0.308	0.335
1991	64	169	9	68	0.288	0.339	0.394
1992	89	184	14	86	0.288	0.327	0.416
1993	78	154	17	86	0.291	0.364	0.445
1994	62	113	6	51	0.304	0.397	0.411
1995	59	132	7	49	0.288	0.341	0.413
Career	**1007**	**2153**	**222**	**1099**	**0.307**	**0.358**	**0.471**

The Simpsons are TM *20th Century Fox*.

THE SEINFELD PHENOMENON

THE SEINFELD PHENOMENON

Mr. Steinbrenner (to George Costanza): Nice to meet you.

George Costanza: Well, I wish I could say the same, but I must say, with all due respect, I find it very hard to see the logic behind some of the moves you have made with this fine organization. In the past twenty years you have caused myself, and the city of New York, a good deal of distress, as we have watched you take our beloved Yankees and reduced them to a laughing stock, all for the glorification of your massive ego!

Mr. Steinbrenner : Hire this man!

George Costanza's *Seinfeld* rant was very memorable and received a large laugh, which was filmed in Los Angeles, a long way from New York. George's diatribe embodied the frustrations of an entire city with some of Steinbrenner's emotion-based decisions which did not seem to most to be for the best of the team.

Ironically, the episode marking Steinbrenner's first appearance is titled "The Opposite," which centers around an emotional, hot-headed George Costanza deciding to curtail his natural instincts and make the opposite choices of what he would naturally do. He is on a job interview with the Yankees and tells off the famously feisty owner with the above tirade as soon as they are introduced.

That's how it all started. George Steinbrenner, the man, became a character depicted, if not caricatured, on the most popular show on all of television, named by *TV Guide* in 2002 as the Greatest Television Program of All Time.

So, the question rises: what the heck is Big Stein doing here? How does a baseball team owner become a fictional character on a hit TV show?

Seinfeld is very much about life in New York City. There are many inside references to specific subway names, businesses, intersections, and restaurants that are meant to capture New York, serving not only as a personal touch to New York residents but to share the unique experience with the rest of the country. At that time, no one could claim more sports headlines in New York than George Steinbrenner, resulting in both his wise moments and his eccentric battles with the players, the managers, the league, and the press. Bringing him into the show and calling him by name fit perfectly into the *Seinfeld* universe that made a certain real-life soup restaurant and nothing-special coffee shop into tourist landmarks.

Despite popular opinion and urban myth, George Steinbrenner only appeared as himself *ONCE* on Seinfeld in the episode “The Invitations”, Season 7 Episode 24. His scenes were cut from the episode and never aired, but they are available on the *Seinfeld* Season 7 Set DVD # 4. Prior to that and in all other Steinbrenner character appearances, two different actors played Steinbrenner on camera, Lee Bear and Mitch Mitchell. Both Bear and Mitchell were only pantomiming while usually being shown from the back of the head, as the voice was provided by none other than series co-creator, writer, and major creative influence, Larry David.

Fans loved the appearances. Steinbrenner the man made for many entertaining moments in reality, but the exaggerated mad-man character portrayed on the show was funny on two levels. It was funny in itself. It was a boss of a big organization acting erratically, which is intrinsically humorous. But, it was even funnier, because Steinbrenner as a character added another layer of realism to the show being set in New York City, and people were well aware of the dictatorial and combative nature of Steinbrenner as New York Yankees team owner. For example, Saddam Hussein was a better subject for parody, a la *South Park*, than another tyrannical ruler who was not as well known. The more well known and eccentric that the figure is, the better the figure is for satire. Steinbrenner certainly met both of these prerequisites.

It is a testament to Big Stein's impact on the Yankees and Major League Baseball that he could garner enough cultural buzz that he would be an ideal candidate to be included in a prime time television sitcom and that a live audience across the country in Los Angeles could recognize both his name and his behavior. How many New Yorker's could recognize the demeanor of the owner of the Los Angeles Dodgers? Furthermore, how many could name him at all?

There was one small problem though. To portray Steinbrenner by name as a recurring character, the *Seinfeld* staff felt they needed his permission.

Originally, they were denied. They were denied on two fronts:

1. He declined the chance to play himself on the show.
2. He denied them permission to make him a character on the show altogether.

According to Larry David, Steinbrenner thought they were ridiculing him. David explained, "He thought we were making fun of him because George [Costanza] was called 'George.' So, he didn't really interpret it the right way. So Jerry had to tell him that 'no, no, no, George, this has nothing to do with you.' So he gave us permission to do it."

One call from Jerry, and things were ready to go.

On the character "Steinbrenner" that they created, Jerry Seinfeld said, "And Larry was so hilarious doing the voice, and he really created this very caricatured, this very mercurial, personality who is just completely all over the place and neurotic…"

Obviously, the character was created as a comic exaggeration of the real-life man and not meant to be a realistic depiction.

But, the big question is, what did Steinbrenner himself think of his depiction on the show?

Well, he obviously thought it wasn't too bad or he would never had agreed to make an appearance on the show himself.

He admits he wasn't the most familiar with the show when he said, "You know, I didn't know the *Seinfeld* show that well. I used to watch it, but I didn't know it that well."

On taking it all in stride, Steinbrenner said during the *Inside Look* on *Seinfeld* Season 5 Disc 4, "If you can't poke fun at yourself, you know, you're not much."

When asked about the accuracy of the portrayal of himself on the show, he responded candidly, "I guess they did a pretty accurate job. Nobody likes to admit they're quite like that, but I guess I was."

Complete Steinbrenner on Seinfeld Episode Guide:

Dan Fathow

1. "The Opposite" Season 5 Episode 22
2. "The Secretary" Season 6 Episode 9
3. "The Race" Season 6 Episode 11
4. "The Jimmy" Season 6 Episode 19
5. "The Wink" Season 7 Episode 4
6. "The Hot Tub" Season 7 Episode 5
7. "The Caddy" Season 7 Episode 12
8. "The Calzone" Season 7 Episode 20
9. "The Bottle Deposit" Part 1 Season 7 Episode 21
10. "The Bottle Deposit" Part 2 Season 7 Episode 22
11. "The Nap" Season 8 Episode 18
12. "The Millennium" Season 8 Episode 20
13. "The Muffin Tops" Season 8 Episode 21
14. "The Finale" Part 1 Season 9 Episode 23
15. "The Finale" Part 2 Season 9 Episode 24

Other Yankee Appearances on Seinfeld

"The Opposite" Season 5 Episode 22

Danny Tartabull

Buck Showalter

Don Mattingly (mentioned, not on camera)

Wade Boggs (mentioned, not on camera)

Luis Polonia (mentioned, not on camera)

Paul O'Neill (mentioned, not on camera)

George Steinbrenner Quotes, Hits, & Legacy

"The Pledge Drive" Season 6 Episode 3

Danny Tartabull

"The Wink" Season 7 Episode 24

Paul O'Neill

"The Abstinence" Season 8 Episode 9

Derek Jeter

Bernie Williams

New York Mets Appearances on Seinfeld

"The Boyfriend" Parts I & II Season 3 Episodes 15 & 16

Keith Hernandez

Roger McDowell

Mookie Wilson (mentioned, not on camera)

Seinfeld is *TM* and intellectual property of Sony Pictures Television and Copyright Castle Rock Entertainment.

CHECK OUT MORE GREAT RELEASES FROM **MEGALODON ENTERTAINMENT LLC**

Follow the **New Orleans Saints** through their amazing **Super Bowl XLIV (44) Championship** season, and re-experience every game, relive every score, and savor every victory. Travel with The Saints on their long, often trying 43 years on the road to success. Compare the stats on every Saints Quarterback. Who has the most yards, wins, and completions? Archie Manning, Drew Brees, Bobby Hebert, or Aaron Brooks? Find out which Saints coach has the best record and the most games. Sean Payton, Jim Mora, or Bum Phillips? This book is the perfect companion for new and long-time Saints fans alike.

ISBN 978-0-9800605-7-7

www.ingramcontent.com/pod-product-compliance
Lightning Source LLC
Chambersburg PA
CBHW072204090426
42740CB00012B/2379
* 9 7 8 1 6 1 5 8 9 0 2 3 1 *